Childre[illegible]
the Worship Service

By David and Sally Michael

Truth:78

And they were bringing children to him
that he might touch them,
and the disciples rebuked them.
[14]But when Jesus saw it, he was indignant
and said to them,
"Let the children come to me;
do not hinder them,
for to such belongs the kingdom of God.
[15]Truly, I say to you,
whoever does not receive the kingdom of God like a child
shall not enter it."
[16]And he took them in his arms and blessed them,
laying his hands on them.

Mark 10:13-16

Children and the Worship Service
by David and Sally Michael

Toll-Free: 1.877.400.1414
info@Truth78.org

Truth:78

www.Truth78.org

Table of Contents

Part 1: Including Children in the Worship Service

Introduction

> ***And they were bringing children to him that he might touch them, and the disciples rebuked them. [14]But when Jesus saw it, he was indignant and said to them, "Let the children come to me; do not hinder them, for to such belongs the kingdom of God. [15]Truly, I say to you, whoever does not receive the kingdom of God like a child shall not enter it."—Mark 10:13-15***

Jesus is still opening His arms and inviting children to come to Him, and one time that happens is when His "Bride" gathers together to worship Him.

It has been more than 50 years since the two of us were "growing up" in the church. At that time, it seemed that most church-going parents and their children understood that they should attend the church service together. None in our circles considered an alternative service for children, or proposed strategies for helping children participate in the worship service…families just did it.

Today in many churches, especially larger ones, the idea of including children in the corporate worship service of the church feels countercultural. How did we get to this point in time when including children in an "adult" worship service seems like a radical idea? In an August 5, 2014 blog post titled, "Sunday Schooling Our Kids Out of Church," Tim Wright gives us part of the answer.

> *About 40 years ago a profound shift took place in many Christian congregations across the country…for all the right reasons…with one troubling unintended consequence: In the 1960's and 1970's, my generation, Baby Boomers, rebelled against the "institutional church" just as we did with every other institution our parents built/supported. We rebelled by dropping out: 2/3rds of my generation dropped out of church.*

In the late 1970's/early 1980's, innovative pastors and congregations of all sizes and denominations looked for ways to draw Boomers back to church. They began to create worship experiences based on the unique "personality" of the Boomer generation. These churches went "contemporary," "seeker," and/or "seeker-friendly." Because these were the primary parenting years for Boomers, these congregations recognized the need to not only provide Boomer-friendly worship experiences for adults, but the need to create dynamic experiences for their children as well, knowing that if the kids wanted to come back, the parents were more likely to come back.

So began a shift from kids worshipping with the big people for one hour followed by all ages attending a second hour of Sunday School, to churches creating Sunday School experiences for kids that ran concurrently with their parents' worship service. In other words, kids and parents were separated from each other, having different Sunday experiences.

Again, the reasons were right...or so we thought. Because these new Boomer services had a sense of evangelism about them (trying to win Boomers back to the church) we didn't want anything to interrupt their focus...like squirming or crying or screaming kids. Church leaders sensed that Boomer parents wanted the one hour break from their kids—that they wanted to focus on their own spiritual life for an hour away from the distraction of their children. And, again, we assumed, reasonably so, that worship targeted to adult boomers would not be all that engaging for kids. So dynamic Sunday school programs were created to engage the kids at their level in their language while their parents were in worship. In fact, some churches didn't (and don't) allow kids into big people worship at all.

The result: Many of these innovated congregations had a positive, significant impact on the lives of disenfranchised Boomers and their kids. Many saw their congregations and their children's ministries grow exponentially. The evangelism imperative to reconnect with Boomers seemed to work. But there was (and is) one huge unintended consequence: We have raised the largest ***unchurched*** *generation in the history of our country.*[1]

Wright's last sentence is startling and sobering. While there are certainly other reasons contributing to the decline in church attendance among young people in our country, there does seem to be a significant connection between the rise of alternative "experiences for kids that ran concurrently with their parents' worship service" and the unprecedented numbers of young people dropping out of church. In our well-intended efforts to reach our children at their level, have we unwittingly hindered our "little ones" from coming to Christ?

Children and the Corporate Gathering of God's People: A Biblical Norm

As we consider the question of children and their participation in the corporate gathering of God's people, it is helpful to observe how the Bible addresses this question, and then how it has been addressed historically in the church.

Not surprisingly, there is very little specific biblical instruction on this topic, most likely because it was a non-issue. The presence of children was assumed whenever the people of God gathered. In his well-researched book, *Children in the Early Church*, Dr. William Strange notes this:

> *...in asking questions about the place of children in the church, we are not going to find out all the answers we might want because we are posing questions about matters which do not seem to have been a problem to the earliest Christians...This does not mean, though, that we can discover nothing at all about children in the early church, only that what we discover will be drawn from inferences or from passing references.*[2]

---

1. Wright, Tim. "Sunday Schooling Our Kids Out of Church," posted August 5, 2014, http://www.patheos.com/blogs/searchingfortomsawyer/2014/08/sunday-schooling-our-kids-out-of-church/ (accessed 7/22/16).
2. Strange, William. A. *Children in the Early Church: Children in the Ancient World, the New Testament and the Early Church.* (Carlisle, United Kingdom: Paternoster Press, 1996), 66.

What we can conclude from these "inferences and passing references" is that children were present, both when Israel gathered in the Old Testament and when the church gathered in the New Testament.

Children and Worship in the Old Testament

We can point to several Old Testament passages that indicate the presence of children in the corporate gathering:

- **Feast of Booths**

  Deuteronomy 31:10-13—And Moses commanded them, "At the end of every seven years, at the set time in the year of release, at the Feast of Booths, [11]when all Israel comes to appear before the LORD your God at the place that he will choose, you shall read this law before all Israel in their hearing. [12]Assemble the people, men, women, and little ones, and the sojourner within your towns, that they may hear and learn to fear the LORD your God, and be careful to do all the words of this law, [13]and that their children, who have not known it, may hear and learn to fear the LORD your God, as long as you live in the land that you are going over the Jordan to possess."

- **Joshua's reading of the Book of the Law after the fall of Ai**

  Joshua 8:34-35—And afterward he read all the words of the law, the blessing and the curse, according to all that is written in the Book of the Law. [35]There was not a word of all that Moses commanded that Joshua did not read before all the assembly of Israel, and the women, and the little ones, and the sojourners who lived among them.

- **Jehoshaphat's call for fasting and prayer**

  2 Chronicles 20:1-4—After this the Moabites and Ammonites, and with them some of the Meunites, came against Jehoshaphat for battle. [2]Some men came

and told Jehoshaphat, "A great multitude is coming against you from Edom, from beyond the sea; and, behold, they are in Hazazon-tamar" (that is, Engedi). [3]Then Jehoshaphat was afraid and set his face to seek the LORD, and proclaimed a fast throughout all Judah. [4]<u>And Judah assembled</u> to seek help from the LORD; from all the cities of Judah they came to seek the LORD.

In this fearful situation where hostile armies are assembling to come against Israel, Jehoshaphat prays the following prayer:

2 Chronicles 20:11-12—"behold, they reward us by coming to drive us out of your possession, which you have given us to inherit. [12]O our God, will you not execute judgment on them? For we are powerless against this great horde that is coming against us. We do not know what to do, but our eyes are on you."

What did the people of Israel do with the children during this prayer service?

2 Chronicles 20:13— Meanwhile all Judah stood before the LORD, <u>with their little ones</u>, their wives, <u>and their children.</u>

Children watched as Jahaziel the priest rose to his feet and said:

2 Chronicles 20:15, 17-18—..."Listen, all Judah and inhabitants of Jerusalem and King Jehoshaphat: Thus says the LORD to you, 'Do not be afraid and do not be dismayed at this great horde, for the battle is not yours but God's....[17]You will not need to fight in this battle. Stand firm, hold your position, and see the salvation of the LORD on your behalf, O Judah and Jerusalem.' Do not be afraid and do not be dismayed. Tomorrow go out against them, and the LORD will be with you." [18]Then Jehoshaphat bowed his head with his face to the ground, and <u>all Judah and the inhabitants of Jerusalem</u> **[we can assume "with their little ones, their wives and**

their children"] ***fell down before the LORD, worshiping the LORD.***

- **Ezra mourning over the faithlessness of the exiles**

  Ezra 10:1—"While Ezra prayed and made confession, weeping and casting himself down before the house of God, a very great assembly of men, women, and children, gathered to him out of Israel, for the people wept bitterly."

- **Nehemiah gathering the people at the Water Gate**

  The wall was completed, and as the people were celebrating the Feast of the Booths, they gathered for a corporate worship service.

  Nehemiah 8:1-3, 6—And all the people gathered as one man into the square before the Water Gate. And they told Ezra the scribe to bring the Book of the Law of Moses that the LORD had commanded Israel. [2]So Ezra the priest brought the Law before the assembly, both men and women and all who could understand what they heard, on the first day of the seventh month. [3]And he read from it facing the square before the Water Gate from early morning until midday, [about 6 hours] ***in the presence of the men and the women and those who could understand. And the ears of all the people were attentive to the Book of the Law...[5]And Ezra opened the book in the sight of all the people, for he was above all the people, and as he opened it all the people stood. [6]And Ezra blessed the LORD, the great God, and all the people answered, "Amen, Amen," lifting up their hands. And they bowed their heads and worshiped the LORD with their faces to the ground.*** [emphasis added]

  Some use the words "all who could understand" to argue that the children were not present, since they were not among those who "could understand." Yet it is likely that they would be present in light of Moses' clear instruction in Deuteronomy 31 (quoted above) regarding children at the Feast of Booths.

Matthew Henry, commenting on Nehemiah 8:1, added this pastoral word to fathers:

Masters of families should bring their families with them to the public worship of God. Women and children have souls to save, and are therefore concerned to acquaint themselves with the word of God and attend on the means of knowledge and grace. Little ones, as they come to the exercise of reason, must be trained up in the exercises of religion.[3]

Children and Worship in the New Testament

Children were clearly present when the crowds gathered around Jesus, and when the early church gathered.

- **Feeding of the 5,000**

  Jesus left by boat to go to "a desolate place by himself." But the crowds learned of it, and when Jesus landed there was a large crowd assembled. There Jesus healed the sick, and most likely taught them as well. Evidently this consumed most of the day (Matthew 14:15—"Now when it was evening… the day is now over") and people were hungry. So Jesus multiplied loaves and fish to feed the crowd—which included children:

  Matthew 14:21—And those who ate were about five thousand men, besides women and children.

- **Teaching regarding the greatest in the kingdom of heaven**

  Matthew 18:1-4—At that time the disciples came to Jesus, saying, "Who is the greatest in the kingdom of heaven?" [2]And calling to him a child, he put him in the midst of them [3]and said, "Truly, I say to you, unless you turn and become like children, you will never enter the kingdom of heaven. [4]Whoever humbles himself like this child is the greatest in the kingdom of heaven." [emphasis added]

---

3. Henry, Matthew. *Matthew Henry's Commentary on the Whole Bible: Complete and Unabridged in One Volume.* (Peabody, Mass.: Hendrickson Publishers, 1994), 634.

- **Jesus welcomed children**

  Matthew 19:13-15—...children were brought to him that he might lay his hands on them and pray. The disciples rebuked the people, [14]but Jesus said, "Let the little children come to me and do not hinder them, for to such belongs the kingdom of heaven." [15]And he laid his hands on them and went away.

- **The Epistles**

  The absence of any specific instruction about children in worship gatherings suggests that it was a non-issue for the early church. We know that Paul intended for his letters to be read to the church when they gathered. Since his instruction in Ephesians 6:1-3 and Colossians 3:20 is directed at children, Paul must have assumed that they would be present to hear the words he directed to them.

  Ephesians 6:1-3—Children, obey your parents in the Lord, for this is right. [2]"Honor your father and mother" (this is the first commandment with a promise), [3]"that it may go well with you and that you may live long in the land."

  Colossians 3:20—Children, obey your parents in everything, for this pleases the Lord.

  Not only does it seem evident that the presence of children in worship is a biblical norm, but we can also conclude that there is no biblical precedent to suggest that children were segregated into age-specific groupings.

Children and the Corporate Gathering of God's People: An Historical Norm

The inclusion of children in the corporate gathering of the church continued beyond the New Testament period, and it seems to have been the norm for the next 1,600 years of church history.

In his article, "Is Age-Integrated Worship a Historical Norm?" Scott Brown stated:

> *...age integration has been the norm in the church, while there have been exceptions and different expressions of it throughout history.*[4]

Scott then offered quotes from three prominent historical figures to reinforce his view:

Martin Luther, 1483-1546

In the publication, *The Table Talk of Martin Luther*, Luther stated:

When I preach, I sink myself deep down. I regard neither doctors nor magistrates, of whom are here in this church above forty; but I have an eye to the multitude of young people, children, and servants, of whom are more than two thousand. I preach to those, directing myself to them that have need thereof. Will not the rest hear me? The door stands open unto them; they may be gone.[5]

John Bunyan, 1628-1688

In his book, *Family Duty: A Father's Duty to His Family*, Bunyan commented on the importance of children being in the worship service:

You should also labor to draw them out to God's public worship, if perhaps God may convert their souls. Said Jacob to his household, and to all that were about him, "Let us arise and go up to Bethel; and I will make there an altar unto God, who answered me in the day of my distress" (Genesis 35:3). Hannah would carry Samuel to Shiloh, that he might abide with God forever (1 Sam. 1:22)...

If they are obstinate, and will not go with you, then bring godly and sound men to your house, and there let the word of God

4. Brown, Scott T. "Is Age-Integrated Worship a Historical Norm?," posted by the National Center for Family-Integrated Churches (NCFIC), February 26, 2016, https://ncfic.org/blog/posts/is_age_integrated_worship_a_historical_norm (accessed 7/22/16).
5. Ibid.

be preached, when you have, as Cornelius, gathered your family and friends together (Acts 10).[6]

Matthew Henry, 1662-1714

In his commentary referring to the passage in 1 Samuel 1:19-28, Henry wrote:

Little children should learn…to worship God. Their parents should instruct them in worship and bring them to it, put them upon engaging in it as well as they can, and God will graciously accept them and teach them to do better.[7]

Likewise in his comments on Luke 2:41-52 regarding Jesus teaching in the temple as a boy, Matthew Henry once again admonishes adults to include children in worship: "It is for the honor of Christ that children should attend on public worship, and he is pleased with their hosannas."[8]

A Philosophical Shift

Four major influences shifted the church's thinking about children in worship.

1. **Sunday School Movement**

   The Sunday school movement unintentionally shifted the weight of responsibility for the spiritual development from the home to the church. It also resulted in the blending of the philosophy of Christian education and public education.

   Robert Raikes (1736-1811) is known as the founder of the Sunday school movement. His hope was to raise the literacy and morality of children in England, focusing on children who at the time were working 12 hours a day or longer in the mills and sweatshops. Their only day off was Sunday, when they were often found running loose in the streets.

---

6. Brown, Scott T. "Is Age-Integrated Worship a Historical Norm?," posted by NCFIC, February 26, 2016, https://ncfic.org/blog/posts/is_age_integrated_worship_a_historical_norm (accessed 7/22/16).
7. Henry, Matthew. *Matthew Henry's Commentary on the Whole Bible: Complete and Unabridged in One Volume.* (Peabody, Mass.: Hendrickson Publishers, 1994).
8. Ibid.

In 1780, Raikes established the first Sunday school in one of the slums of London, seeking to train these children in the basics of education by a network of educators who became their principle teachers. The movement spread like wildfire throughout England, especially among Baptist, Congregational, and Methodist churches. By 1831, Sunday schools in Great Britain were teaching 1.25 million children weekly, approximately 25 percent of the population.

In 1790, the first American Sunday school opened its doors in Philadelphia among the city's poor. It was called the "First Day Society," and it focused on teaching reading and writing, and the formation of moral consciousness.

During the first few decades of the Sunday school movement, it would have been unheard of and considered inappropriate for children of Christian parents active in the church to participate in Sunday schools. However, the rise of industrialization in America and England changed this. Fathers began working outside the home environment to gain higher wages and more opportunities in the city.[9] This resulted in fathers having less time with their children and, consequently less involvement in their discipleship. As opportunities for spiritual instruction at home were diminishing, Sunday schools were moving from the streets; churches adopted the model for the religious education of children in the church.

2. The Shift to Age-Specific

John D. Philbrick (1818-1886) was a prominent American educator and frequent contributor to educational journals. Faced with overcrowded classrooms and disorder, his solution was to reorganize the classroom structure, grouping students according to age. With each age group in a separate, self-contained classroom with its own teacher, the problem of overcrowded classrooms would be solved with order and discipline established in schools. To this end, he co-founded the Quincy School in Boston, America's first 12-room schoolhouse, which became the standard for education in America.

---

9. Roberts, Paul, and Bill Moseley. "Father's Time." *Psychology Today*. May 1, 1996. https://www.psychologytoday.com/articles/199605/fathers-time (accessed 10/12/16).

As with the Sunday school movement, there is much that can be said about the impact this has had on Christian education, but a regrettable byproduct of these two influences is that the church began adapting Christian education philosophy, curriculum development, and even architecture to this new standard.

By the 1940s, the age-segregated mindset was fully integrated into the mainstream of church life and began influencing the perception of children's participation in the worship service. Expecting children to sit through an "adult" service started making less sense, and thus children's church started appearing alongside Sunday school as an institution in the church.

3. **The Establishment of Adolescence as a Significant Developmental Stage**

   G. Stanley Hall (1844-1924) was an American psychologist and educator who focused on childhood development and evolutionary theory. He popularized the term "adolescence" and linked this stage of development to:

   - conflict with parents,
   - mood disruptions,
   - and risky behavior.[10]

   Over time, this thinking lead to the perception of a fixed life stage between childhood and adulthood around which a "teen culture" emerged.

   By the 1950s, there was increasing emphasis on teen evangelism, and a number of parachurch youth organizations and clubs were founded, such as Youth for Christ, Child Evangelism, Pioneer Girls, Christian Service Brigade, Young Life, Awana, and Royal Ambassadors.

   With the increasing emphasis on youth ministry inside the church, the addition of full-time staff to develop and sustain that ministry became the norm in many churches. Priority

10. Vitelli, Romeo, PhD. "Storming into Adulthood," www.psychologytoday.com/blog/media-spotlight/201309/storming-adulthood (accessed 7/22/16).

was given to doing whatever it took to attract and retain the youth, and the youth group became the focal point of participation for youth in the church. Thus the youth, especially in larger churches, were often separated from the rest of the church, cloistered within their own age-segregated gatherings.

The church, along with parents, lost sight of the responsibility to impart the "full counsel of God" to the next generation. The concept of systematic instruction and spiritual development rarely went beyond the basic "Gospel message." Consequently, Baby Boomers, for the most part, grew up without a biblical worldview and the biblical foundation to interpret the cultural revolution of the 1960s that defied just about every institutional and social norm, including the church.

As the Baby Boomers outgrew their youth group and stepped into the next life stage, they had little reason for staying connected with the local church, which led to aging congregations and a sharp decline in church attendance.

4. The Pursuit of "Unchurched Harry"

In the 1980s, a movement within the church emerged to win Baby Boomers back to church. The average Baby Boomer was defined as "Unchurched Harry."[11] Intentional efforts were launched to persuade "Harry" to give the church another try. The church worked hard to remove the many obstacles that were keeping "Harry" away from the church, and ultimately from the Gospel. The goal was to create an atmosphere that would be as welcoming, comfortable, pleasant and worthwhile to the unchurched as possible. This included freeing these young adults in the '80s from the responsibility and distraction of their children by providing a separate experience that was as positive and as engaging for the children as the experience was for their parents.

---

11. We were first introduced to "Unchurched Harry" on an audio recording of Bill Hybels describing the ministry philosophy of Willow Creek Church. Hybels' long-time associate, Lee Strobel, subsequently wrote a book titled, *Inside the Mind of Unchurched Harry & Mary: How to Reach Friends and Family Who Avoid God and the Church.* (Grand Rapids, Mich.: Zondervan, 1993).

The strategy worked. Boomers were making their way back to church. They heard the Gospel and came to Christ. The church grew, and ministry to children, youth, and families became a crucial component of the infrastructure that supported the mission of the church. Budgets, staffing, and accommodations for children were enlarged. Like the growth of youth ministry in the '40s and '50s, we witnessed unprecedented development and expansion of children and family ministries in the church.

In his August 5, 2014 blog post, after pointing out that this successful effort resulting in "the largest **unchurched** generation in the history of our country," Pastor Tim Wright admits that "there are many reasons why each generation in our culture is increasingly distanced from the church. Some have to do with societal shifts that have nothing to do with the church. Some have to do with the inability of the church to articulate the Gospel in compelling ways."[12]

But then Wright wonders if one of the reasons is because we "have shifted kids out of the main worship experience, enculturated them in their own program, and robbed them of any touchpoints with the rest of the body of Christ. Another way of saying it: by segregating our kids out of worship, we never assimilated them into the life of the congregation. They had no touch points. They had no experience. They had no connection with the main worship service—its liturgy, its music, its space, its environment, and its adults. It was a foreign place to them. And so...once they finished with the kids/or youth program, they left the church."[13]

He concludes with these remarks: "With good intentions we attempted to raise kids to be Christians, but we didn't raise them to be Churched Christians. And perhaps that, in part, is why so few of them attend a church today."[14]

---

12. Wright, Tim. "Sunday Schooling Our Kids Out of Church," posted August 5, 2014, http://www.patheos.com/blogs/searchingfortomsawyer/2014/08/sunday-schooling-our-kids-out-of-church/ (accessed 7/22/16).
13. Ibid.
14. Ibid.

Leaders concerned about this disturbing trend are wisely challenging and encouraging parents to bring their children into the corporate worship service, and some like Tim Wright (quoted earlier) are going a step further by dispensing with Sunday school programs for children. As eager as we are for families to worship together, and as much as we emphasize the importance of parents assuming the primary responsibility for the discipleship of their children, we believe that Sunday school has an important place in the church. If, for some reason, parents must choose between Sunday school and the worship service, we advise them to choose the worship service. However, we hasten to emphasize that Sunday school can be a helpful structure for the systematic biblical, doctrinal, theological discipleship of our children, and we encourage children to attend both worship services and Sunday school. Sunday school should complement, reinforce and support—but not replace—parental instruction and the corporate gathering of God's people in worship.

Why Children Should Participate When the Church Gathers for Worship

There are four important reasons why it is beneficial for children to attend the worship service of the church.

1. **There is spiritual benefit for children who participate in the worship service.** This is the most important reason to encourage the participation of children in the worship service. Though some elements of the service may not be fully understood by children, the reality is that there are inescapable spiritual realities present in the corporate gathering of God's people. Some of these include:

   The Holy Spirit is present when the church is gathered.

   Matthew 18:20—"For where two or three are gathered in my name, there am I among them."

   Children have come to faith sitting through a worship service. They can experience the conviction of the Spirit and the presence of God in a church service, even though they cannot understand all the words of a song or sermon.

God is not hindered by the maturity or cognitive development of a child. God can move in the hearts of the very young, even when something isn't "age appropriate."

John 16:13a—When the Spirit of truth comes, he will guide you into all the truth...

The Word of God is powerful, and it has influence over any "soul and spirit."

Hebrews 4:12—*[The Word]** ***is living and active, sharper than any two-edged sword, piercing to the division of soul and of spirit, of joints and of marrow, and discerning the thoughts and intentions of the heart.

There are intangible aspects in the service that children sense and learn from, even if they are not understanding all the words. Earnestness, bigness, seriousness, joy, and the intensity experienced in the worship service communicates that what is being talked about or sung about is really important.

John Piper has stated this point well:

There is a sense of solemnity and awe which children should experience in the presence of God. This is not likely to happen in children's church. Is there such a thing as children's thunder or children's lightning or the crashing of the sea "for children"?

A deep sense of the unknown and the mysterious can rise in the soul of a sensitive child in solemn worship—if his parents are going hard after God themselves. A deep moving of the magnificence of God can come to the young, tender heart through certain moments of great hymns or "loud silence" or authoritative preaching. These are of immeasurable value in the cultivation of a heart that fears and loves God.[15]

15. Piper, John and Noël. "The Family: Together in God's Presence," January 1, 1996, http://www.desiringGod.org/articles/the-family-together-in-gods-presence (accessed 7/22/16). See Appendix for the complete text of this article.

Children learn more than we think they do.

Again John Piper instructs us:

Children absorb a tremendous amount that is of value. And this is true even if they say they are bored...Music and words become familiar. The message of the music starts to sink in. The form of the service comes to feel natural. The choir makes a special impression with a kind of music the children may hear at no other time. Even if most of the sermon goes over their heads, experience shows that children hear and remember remarkable things.[16]

2. **Attending the worship service involves children in the most central, most regular, most valuable, and most corporate activity of the church.** When we encourage families to worship together, we communicate to the children that they are a part of the congregation and, as such, should be included when the church gathers to worship. The presence of children also serves as a reminder to the church of its responsibility to nurture the faith of the next generation

   The exclusion of children can foster a detachment from the church and leave them with little reason to be involved after they've outgrown the specialized programs for children and youth. Good habits and spiritual disciplines that are established in childhood are more likely to continue into adulthood. In fact, evidence suggests children who grow up attending the corporate worship services with their parents are more likely to continue active church involvement after they leave home.

   John Piper notes that children who grow up regularly attending the worship service, "…unless we teach them otherwise, will grow up thinking: 'This is where I belong on Sunday morning…' It will never enter their heads that not being there is a possibility if we expect it of them."[17]

---

16. Piper, John and Noël. "The Family: Together in God's Presence," January 1, 1996, http://www.desiringGod.org/articles/the-family-together-in-gods-presence (accessed 7/22/16). See Appendix for the complete text of this article.
17. Piper, John. "The Children, The Church, and the Chosen," Sunday evening sermon at Bethlehem Baptist Church of Minneapolis, Minnesota on September 22, 1980, http://www.desiringGod.org/messages/the-children-the-church-and-the-chosen (accessed 7/22/16).

John Piper continues:

We do not believe that children who have been in children's church for several years between the ages of 6 and 12 will be more inclined or better trained to enjoy worship than if they had spent those years at the side of their parents. In fact, the opposite is probably the case.

It will probably be harder to acclimate a 10- or 12-year-old to a new worship service than a 5- or 6-year-old. The cement is much less wet, and vast possibilities of shaping the impulses of the heart are gone.[18]

In an article entitled, "Children in Worship—Let's Bring it Back," Jason Helopoulos states the following:

Teenagers in our culture often balk at attending corporate worship. But how many of our teenagers have we setup for this reaction, because we did not consistently include them in worship until they were a teenager? If attending church for years has always meant coloring Bible pictures, singing songs to a cd, playing games, and doing crafts—then we should not be surprised that our young people find worship to be odd, uncomfortable, and even boring. I love good children's songs—they ring through my house. I love good children's Christian crafts—they decorate my study. But if this alone is the rhythm of church life we have set up for our children week in and week out, we have done them a great disservice.

They must see, know, and learn that the singing of the great hymns of the faith, the preaching of the Word, reading of confessions, corporate prayers, etc. is anything but boring. It is the gathered life of the community of faith. It is our weekly rhythm—appointed by God, designed by Him, established for the ages—this is what we want them to know, because we want them to know and worship Him.[19]

---

18. Piper, John and Noël. "The Family: Together in God's Presence," January 1, 1996, http://www.desiringGod.org/articles/the-family-together-in-gods-presence (accessed 7/22/16).
19. Helopoulos, Jason. "Children in Worship–Let's Bring it Back," posted by Kevin DeYoung on March 6, 2012, https://blogs.thegospelcoalition.org/kevindeyoung/?s=children+in+worship--let%27s+bring+it+back (accessed 7/22/16).

As John Piper has so aptly said:

Worship is the most valuable thing a human can do. The cumulative effect of 650 worship services spent with Mom and Dad between the ages of 4 and 17 is incalculable.[20]

3. **It provides children with an intergenerational experience and thus the opportunity to be influenced and benefit from the example of others, especially their parents.**

We want our children to establish a habit of worship attendance, but more than that, we want them to *delight* in worshipping God. To that end, our example has a powerful influence on our children. For better or for worse, our children will take their cues from us.

Our children are more likely to cherish the worship of God if they witness that heart for worship in us. When they see their parents and other adults bow their heads in earnest prayer, or lift their hands in praise, the genuine worship they observe can stir their hearts to worship. Children can observe parents listening intently, taking notes, and processing the truth they are hearing. They observe this hunger for the Word of God, which can stir their own hearts to hunger for God's Word.

How might the heart of a little girl be stirred when she looks up and sees her mother worshipping God with singing and tears flowing down her cheeks? How might the soul of a boy be influenced as he observes his father week after week bowing in prayer after a word of challenge or exhortation from the pastor? Can we measure the impact on a child who sees an elderly man put his gift in the offering plate week after week, or observes his pastor's passion as he preaches the truths of the Word?

Jason Helopoulos reinforces this point with these words:

What a benefit there is when children witness their mother or father singing with conviction, praying in reverence, listening intently to the sermon, or receiving the Lord's Supper in joy. In

20. Wright, Tim. "Sunday Schooling Our Kids Out of Church," posted August 5, 2014, http://www.patheos.com/blogs/searchingfortomsawyer/2014/08/sunday-schooling-our-kids-out-of-church/ (accessed 7/22/16).

these moments a child witnesses the importance of faith and worship. There are few greater encouragements to a child's faith then seeing their parents worship God with reverence and joy.[21]

Pastor Bud Burk also emphasizes what children observe when they are in worship with their parents:

[They are] *watching your silent attention to the heralding of the Word of God. Watching you smile when the pastor says something that encourages your heart or watching you nod when you say, "Yes, that's right." Or watching you shake your head with a countenance of sadness. "Why is Mommy sad?" Maybe it is conviction of the Holy Spirit.* [A] *child sees years of this, week after week, month after month; watching you read your Bible as the preacher preaches—sees you open up your Bible. Watching you look up when the pastor's voice gets really loud. Having an effect on a child's spiritual growth even though the child may not be able to say what the pastor just said. Or years of watching the pastor smile with joy or have an earnest look on his face; or years of watching you sing. Watching you raise your hands. Means something to them because it means something to you. Watching Mom sit down when everyone else is singing, when everyone else is standing, and watching her put her head down and watching Dad put his hand on her shoulder. No words, just a moment that has an incredible effect on children.*

Years watching you eat the Lord's supper. Years of watching you hold the cup and look at it. Or years of watching you hold the bread—Jesus' body being pierced. They see. Watching your eyes close during most of the Lord's supper devotional or song. Parents' silence has an impact.[22]

4. It facilitates the discipleship of our children.

---

21. Helopoulos, Jason. "Children in Worship–Let's Bring it Back," posted by Kevin DeYoung, March 6, 2012, http://thegospelcoalition.org/blogs/kevindeyoung (accessed 7/22/16).
22. Burk, Bud. "The Generations in the Worship Service," seminar delivered at a conference in 2013 held by Truth78 (then called Children Desiring God). Audio recording at http://ethomasmedia.com/cdg/audio/2013Conference/Burk_Generations.mp3 (accessed 7/22/16).

Bringing children into the worship service provides an opportunity for them to learn how to worship God and to discover the purpose for which they were created. Lord willing, not only will our children worship God here on earth, but will spend eternity doing so.

Children can be taught to listen and engage with what is being said even if they do not understand everything. Drawing pictures of what they hear from the preacher, listening for specific words, writing down the words they don't understand or questions they have, or recording something they learned about God are all ways children can learn to be attentive listeners and interact with the Word being proclaimed. The content of prayers, songs, and sermons give parents the opportunity to discuss, explain, and teach truths to their children. Children do understand great truths from the sermon and can become astute students of the Word, especially if they are trained to listen well.

Children also learn how to sit quietly and to submit to their parents during a worship service as explained by John Piper:

> *...the desire to have children in the worship service is part of a broader concern that children be reared so that they are "submissive and respectful in every way" (1 Timothy 3:4). To sit still and be quiet for an hour or two on Sunday is not an excessive expectation for a healthy 6-year-old who has been taught to obey his parents. It requires a measure of discipline, but that is precisely what we want to encourage parents to impart to their children in the first five years.*[23]

---

23. Piper, John and Noël. "The Family: Together in God's Presence," published January 1, 1996, http://www.desiringGod.org/articles/the-family-together-in-gods-presence (accessed 7/22/16).

Part 2: Strategies for Involving Children in the Worship Service

Usually the first question asked regarding the topic of children attending the worship service is, "At what age do you include children in the church service?" Although there is no magical age, there are some considerations worth noting.

In an article titled "Mom Tested Tips," Jason Helopoulos makes this observation:

> *Many believe that it is harder to introduce a five year old to corporate worship than a twelve year old, but this is not true. A five year old is in the formative years of training. They are not yet 'set in their ways.' A few months of struggling with a four or five year old teaching them how to sit in corporate worship yields benefits for the rest of their lives.*[24]

The key concern about when to encourage children to attend the church service is to engage children young enough that attending church is part of the rhythm of life; it is a habit formed in the early years. Our experience has been that upon graduation from nursery, at preschool age (three or four), children then attend the service.[25] By five years old, an appropriately disciplined child should be able to sit through a church service.

Some churches provide childcare for children older than five years, which is at times prompted by the reluctance of parents to bring their children to church services. Some parents object to bringing their young children to services because of the behavior battles they face. Though it may be distracting and, at times, frustrating to train a young child to sit quietly and attentively, this is one of the tasks a child must learn.

---

24. Helopoulos, Jason. "Children in Worship—Mom Tested Tips," posted on March 7, 2012, http://blogs.thegospelcoalition.org/kevindeyoung/2012/03/07/children-in-worship-mom-tested-tips/ (accessed 7/22/16).
25. In our years at Bethlehem Baptist Church of Minneapolis, Minnesota, children were graduated if they had reached three years old by September. Those who turned three after September would wait until the following September to graduate to the preschool Sunday school department. This kept the children in the same grade as they were in school.

In the article, "The Family Together in God's Presence" John and Noël Piper make this point:

> *To sit still and quiet for an hour or two on Sunday is not an excessive expectation for a healthy 6-year old who has been taught to obey his parents. It requires a measure of discipline but that is precisely what we want to encourage parents to impart to their children in the first five years. Thus the desire to have children in the worship service is part of a broader concern that children be reared so that they are "submissive and respectful in every way" (1 Timothy 3:4). Children can be taught in the first five years of life to obey their father and mother when they say, "Sit still and be quiet." Parents' helplessness to control their children should not be solved by alternative services but by a renewal of discipline in the home.*[26]

It does seem that in this age where permissive parenting has such a strong influence on young parents, the Pipers have given appropriate counsel regarding the need to discipline children, rather than accommodate them. The calling of church leaders is not to lead young parents in what is easier for families, but rather in what is better.

A study done more than two decades ago determined that children who attend Sunday school but do not attend the church service are more likely not to attend church as adults. Conversely, children who attend the church service but not Sunday school are more likely to attend church as adults, as are those who attend both Sunday school and church.[27]

---

26. Piper, John and Noël. "The Family: Together in God's Presence," January 1, 1996, http://www.desiringGod.org/articles/the-family-together-in-gods-presence (accessed 7/22/16).
27. Wright, Tim. "Sunday Schooling Our Kids Out of Church," posted August 5, 2014, http://www.patheos.com/blogs/searchingfortomsawyer/2014/08/sunday-schooling-our-kids-out-of-church/ (accessed 7/22/16).

Parental Strategies for Effectively Engaging Children in Corporate Worship Gatherings

- **Responsibility**—Recognize that it is our job as parents to train our children to sit in the service. It takes effort and sacrifice. There will be times when we will be interrupted by our children and not able to concentrate as much as we would if our children were not with us. We must keep in mind that this season of child training is for a relatively short time, and God will give us the grace and wisdom to navigate this season as we depend on Him.
- **Training**—Acknowledge that helping our children participate in the church service requires training. Right attitudes and behavior usually develop gradually. We should expect it to take a few months for a young child to participate in the church service and look forward to being there. As we train our children with faith and patience and consistency, they will learn—eventually.

  It is important that we train our child in an understanding way. Our expectations for our children should be realistic. For some children, it can be very difficult to sit quietly for an extended period of time. Other children will catch on quickly. We must recognize that children are different and thank God for the unique personality He has given to each child.

  When possible, it is helpful to find a place to sit where a child is not easily distracted...or can easily distract others. Some parents find that sitting near the front is helpful because there are less distractions for the child, although it may be a longer way to the exit if a parent needs to leave with the child.

  When training an active young child, a parent may need to remove the child partway through the service. This can help the child have success by not pressing him beyond his limit. A parent may need to start with a 10-minute limit for a very young child, and then gradually stretch the time until the child can sit through the whole service.

In applying this strategy, we must be careful not to reinforce bad behavior. Some children may discover that by misbehaving during the service they get to leave the service and are free to run around in another room. Children should be regularly reminded of our expectations, and if we remove them from the service we should take them to a place where they can sit quietly, perhaps continue to listen to the service and not distract others.

Parents with multiple children may want to invite a grandparent or good friend to help. This can be a wonderful opportunity for the body to minister to young families. Perhaps there is a widow or a single person who would welcome the opportunity to participate in worship with your family.

It is also helpful to take advantage of other opportunities during the week to train children to sit quietly and listen attentively, such as waiting for an appointment or during a story time at your local library. Worshipping at home provides a great opportunity for training our children to worship at church. Children who participate in family worship will more quickly adapt to listening to the reading of the Word, concentrating during prayer, and singing during worship.

- **Preparation—**Sunday morning starts on Saturday night. Setting out clothes and shoes, getting the offering ready, packing totes and even getting a head start on Sunday dinner can help prepare us and our children for worship and minimize the stress of Sunday morning. When Sunday morning arrives, enjoy a simple breakfast and leave plenty of margin in the Sunday morning schedule for the unexpected. Before the service, it is helpful for parents to take young children to the restroom and remind them that they will "not be able to leave the service because we don't want to miss any part of it."
- **Pray—**It is important that we not neglect to seek God's help to make this time a valuable part of spiritual training for our children. We want to pray for their hearts, and that they will see God as the greatest treasure and truly worship Him.

- **Expectations**—We want to be sure to remind our children of our expectations for their behavior during the church service. This is a time to participate in singing and praying, and for them to quietly listen. These expectations should be clear and rehearsed often, especially in the beginning of the training process.

  Be proactive by talking through the service ahead of time. If there is a baptism during the service, explain what will happen and the meaning behind it. Similarly, when the Lord's Supper is celebrated, help explain its meaning and significance, as well as any expectations you have of your child during that part of the service. Young children will need to understand that they should not take the "cracker and juice" when it goes by, but to anticipate the time when they will be able to participate in communion with the rest of the church.

- **Model**—It is important that we be role models for our children. We should begin the Lord's Day with a positive attitude, a cheerful tone, a spirit of anticipation and enthusiasm, and a heart for worship. Our singing should be heartfelt and authentic. Our hearts should be engaged in corporate prayer, and we should be attentive and actively listening when the Word of God is preached. Genuine worship is contagious, and our children will benefit when they witness us genuinely and authentically engaged in worship.
- **Instruction**—If the church provides a worship folder or posts the order of service on its website, it is helpful if children can be acquainted with the various parts of the service ahead of time. Reading the sermon passage and talking about its meaning at home makes it more familiar to the child and can help them connect with the sermon.

  Since singing is such a significant part of most worship services, children, especially pre-readers, are more likely to participate when they are familiar with the worship songs. Even if they cannot learn the whole hymn or song, we can teach them a portion of it and alert them when the portion they know is about to be sung.

Again, we should not neglect to pray with our children before the service starts, together asking the Lord for grace to behave in a manner that honors Christ and for the help of the Holy Spirit to give an understanding of God's truth and a heart of worship.

- **Participation**—Remember that we are not just training our children to sit quietly and behave in church. We are training them to worship the Lord. Children should be encouraged to participate in as much of the service as they can. Instruction at home can make a big difference in a child's participation on Sunday morning.

  We should aim to provide our children with a repertoire of the hymns and choruses that are sung during the worship services. Encourage children to participate when the congregation is singing, and not just silently look around. If the congregation is singing from a hymn book or participating in a corporate reading, it is helpful if children, especially pre-readers, can follow along with an adult pointing out the words as they are being sung or spoken. This helps capture a child's attention and draw him into worship.

  Children should be taught to stand when the rest of the congregation is standing, to clap when the congregation is encouraged to clap, and to bow their heads when the congregation is praying. We need to help children understand why participation in corporate worship is important and teach them how to be active participants, rather than passive observers.

  Even though we want to minimize conversation with children during the service, we can use transition moments to help them stay engaged by offering a brief explanation or by encouraging the child's faith, saying something like, "I love this verse," or "I love what this song says about God."

  The offering time is another opportunity for children and adults to participate. We want children to understand that this portion of the worship service is more than a convenient time to collect donations for the church. Psalm 96:8 says, "Ascribe to the LORD the glory due his name; bring an offering, and come into his courts!" Bringing an offering is an opportunity for us and our children to honor Christ as our greater treasure, and to affirm with our brothers and sisters in Christ that "Some trust in chariots and some in horses, but we trust in the name of the LORD our God" (Psalm 20:7). We want to help our children see this moment in the service as an opportunity to express to the Lord that we trust Him to care for us and want to be a part of His work in the world.

As convenient as online giving may be, we may want to make the effort to bring our offering into the worship service so that our children follow our example of regular and faithful worship in this tangible way. It is best when children can contribute their own money. Even though younger children have a limited understanding of the value of money, parents can teach them proportional giving by providing them with a small allowance in coins that can be easily allocated to different categories (offering, savings, spending, etc.).

- **Focused Listening**—The worship service gives us an opportunity to help our children develop the discipline of active listening, especially when the Word of God is preached. Over time, we want our children to learn how to focus their attention on the sermon. In the beginning it can be helpful to whisper simple instructions, such as, "Listen to this story," or "Can you draw a picture of what the pastor is talking about?" or "When you hear the pastor say [this word], draw a star on your paper."

  Drawing and coloring are activities that children enjoy and are usually not distracting to others. By encouraging children to listen carefully to what the pastor is saying and then draw what they hear, we are teaching them to be active listeners. However, giving our children paper and crayons without directing them to connect what they hear with what they draw is actually teaching them to tune out and disengage from this central part of the worship service.

  Books are also helpful for occupying younger children with shorter attention spans. Choose books that will not be distracting[28] and will direct them to God or His Word (Bible storybooks, etc.), so that even if the child cannot stay engaged with the sermon the whole time, he is learning that this is the time when we focus on God and His Word, not on cars, trucks, and superheroes.

As children mature and learn how to write, note-taking becomes another opportunity for them to listen carefully and engage with what they are hearing. It is helpful if they can observe and even copy their parents' notes into their own special worship notebook. Truth78 offers a special worship notebook for elementary-age children called the *My Church Notebook.*[29]

It is also helpful for each child to have special worship tote bag that can include a children's Bible, Bible storybooks, a pad of paper or notebook, Bible story coloring books (e.g., *He Established a Testimony* or *He Has Spoken By His Son*),[30] or the *Fighter Verses Coloring Book*,[31] and Crayola Twistable™ crayons or colored pencils.[32]

- **Encouragement**—We want the worship experience to be as positive as it can be for our children, so it is important that we be alert to specific ways to encourage them. It encourages them when we acknowledge and express our delight in their singing, their good behavior, their friendliness to others, or something they draw or write in their notebook. Let them hear us express what a blessing it is to be able to worship together and to have them in the service with us.

  We should recognize that the average church service will seem long to young children. It may seem to them that like the sermon will never end, and we should not be surprised or

28. Small books that have pages that can be easily and quietly turned can be less distracting than large books. Obviously, books that produce sounds will be distracting as well.
29. Available from Truth78 (Truth78.org).
30. Ibid.
31. Ibid.
32. The Crayola Twistable™ crayons tend to be less messy than other crayons, and the Crayola Twistable™ colored pencils do not need to be sharpened. Markers tend to smell and squeak, and can be more distracting to others. They can also leak, and it is easier to mark clothing, cushions, and other items with them.

alarmed if they tell us they are bored in church.[33] It is reasonable for a young child to feel this way, and we should be careful to acknowledge and even validate these feelings. We do not serve the children and our desires for them when we deny these understandable feelings or reprimand them for being bored.

Instead we want to deal with our children in an understanding way. We can acknowledge that the service is long for a child, and that the pastor uses many words that are difficult for them to understand. We can also be quick to acknowledge that we are not bored in the service because we understand the big words. Assure them that, in time, it will become easier for them to sit still, understand, and be interested in more of the preaching. Encourage children to be patient, participate, and gain as much as they can from the service.

- **Discipline**—Even though sitting quietly for an extended time can be difficult, we should expect children to be as obedient and submissive to their parents during the church service as at any other time. Ignoring or neglecting to correct disobedience and misbehavior during the service can hinder a child from benefitting from the service and will undermine our discipleship efforts. Children should expect to be corrected during the church service, and parents must be careful not to give in to the fear that disciplining a child for misbehaving in church will cause a child to dislike church. Rather, we must do what is best for our children, recognizing that they need to learn to be under authority and to be obedient.

  A parent may need to remove a child from the service to keep from disturbing others and to provide proper correction. With consistency and patience, a parent should not need to do this too many times before a child learns and submits to what is expected during the service.

33. Many parents are concerned when their children are "bored." But being bored is part of life for a child as he matures and learns to adapt to different environments and situations.

- **Review**—Children will often follow the example of their parents, which is why we want to be careful to speak positively about the service on the way home. It is helpful for them to hear their parents and others talk about the moments in the service or the points in the pastor's message that were especially meaningful or helpful. Let our children hear how we were affected by the service and how God spoke through His Word. Our children should be encouraged to ask questions, share their impressions, and discuss what they learned and the specific ways that God may have spoken to them. Take some time to look at their drawings or their notes. Make comments and ask questions so that children understand that their efforts to participate in the service are important and appreciated.
- **Relax**—Sometimes parents are reluctant to take their child to the service for fear of being embarrassed or judged by their child's misbehavior. We must keep in mind that all children are sinners, just like the grown-ups sitting around them. We should not be surprised that sin nature expresses itself in the misbehavior of a child. By God's grace, our children will learn submission to their parents and ultimately submission to Christ once they are born again.

  Rather than being annoyed by a child's misbehavior or inwardly critical of parents, those sitting nearby can be silently praying that the child's heart will be inclined to the Lord, and that the parents will have the wisdom and patience they need to deal with their child's behavior and faithfully lead their child to walk in God's ways.

  Our ultimate desire as parents is to please the Lord...and not to perform for others. We will not handle every situation perfectly, but by God's grace our children will mature in faith, grow to be like Christ, and worship the Lord with all their hearts in church on Sunday morning, and one day in the very presence of the King of Kings.

May God bless your efforts to disciple your children and bring them into the presence of the living God.

You make known to me the path of life;
in your presence there is fullness of joy;
at your right hand are pleasures forevermore.
—Psalm 16:11

Part 3: For Leaders

Leadership Suggestions for Casting a Vision of Including Children in the Worship Service

In addition to the need for parents to understand their responsibility to introduce their children to the worship service, the congregation and the church leaders must also understand their corporate responsibility for the faith of the next generation. Very often the vision for welcoming children into the church service must come from the pastor or minister for children. After giving a prayer-soaked, well thought out biblical rational of the importance of children attending the corporate gathering, it may be necessary to continue to patiently and winsomely teach, encourage, and support parents and church leaders.

1. **Pray that God would open a door for children in your worship services.** God can accomplish in 30 seconds what would take more than a lifetime of striving. Bathe all your efforts in prayer, recognizing both the power of God to change hearts and the desire of God to create worshippers in the next generation.

2. **Be careful and sensitive. Proceed with patience, winsomeness, and grace.** There are reasons why some people believe children should not be present in the worship service. Some of these are more legitimate than others. Some people value the undistracted hearing of the Gospel, or they sincerely hold the conviction that children benefit more in a ministry tailored to their unique stage in life. Parents can feel threatened when faced with having their children's behavior on display to the church. There is also a respectful desire that parents have of others, not wanting them to be distracted by children. Regardless of the reason, we must sensitively and patiently cast a vision for those who do not understand the value of having children in the service.

3. **Begin with vision.** Cast a vision for integrating children into not only the church service, but into the life of the church in multiple venues. Help the adults to see both the value and

the responsibility of incorporating children into the teaching and activity of the church.

4. **Educate the congregation and the parents.** Cultivate sensitivity and patience in the congregation as they support parents in nurturing the faith of their children. Cultivate in the parents a sensitivity toward the needs of those around them to be able to worship and listen to the Word without undue frustration and distraction.

5. **Take a long view and be satisfied to make "baby steps" in the right direction.** It is better to first win people to your point of view than to force it upon them by taking away options or creating rules. Persuasion usually is more effective than coercion.

   Give the fathers in the congregation a two-fold challenge—to worship with their families at home and to worship together at church as a family. Affirm, encourage, and support parents who are bringing children into the service; and begin to train and encourage the congregation about their responsibility to disciple the next generation. Individuals in the congregation can be challenged to help a family with multiple children by sitting with them and helping their children to focus. Congregation members can be encouraged to pray for the children around them, accepting with grace squirmy and distracting children who are learning to sit in the service.

   Encourage up-front leaders to occasionally acknowledge the children in the room by including them in comments, or defining a word for them. If the leadership includes the children in the service, the congregation will more likely catch the vision to include them as well.

   If it is too significant of a leap for parents or leadership to accept the idea of children in worship, consider making incremental steps to this end, such as including the children for special services, or on a once-a-quarter basis, or during the summer months.

Leadership Suggestions for including Children in the Worship Services

The following list includes some practical suggestions leaders can incorporate to encourage families to worship together and to make the church service a positive and meaningful experience for children.

- Pray that God will open the hearts and minds of the leaders and parents of the church to see how important it is that children attend the worship service.

  The following counsel by John Bunyan is as crucial today as it was in his day: "You can do more than pray, after you have prayed, but you cannot do more than pray until you have prayed."

- Be consciously aware that there are children present and include them in comments from the pulpit or during the worship time.

  All of us have probably been in the situation of being a newcomer among friends who have known each other for years. When they start talking about shared experiences, it is natural to feel on the "outside." However, the feeling of being an outsider dissipates when there is a sensitive person who will pause in the conversation to include you with some background information so you can follow the conversation and not feel excluded. It is not necessary to do this often; an occasional comment can help you to feel that "this gathering is for me, too."

  At times, pastors can do this from the pulpit by defining a difficult word or calling something to the children's attention, such as "Kids, if you are drawing pictures of the sermon..." or "Children, listen to this; it is really important..."

  This need not be frequent, but an occasional comment remembering children is helpful. When we notice children in this way, they will not only feel included, but they will often work a little harder at understanding what is going on.

  Children love challenges! And they love it when someone thinks they can do something that seems hard. Much of the content of the sermons are above the cognitive ability of young children, but not all of it, and if a child is challenged to listen and try to understand, he will glean truth from the sermon.

- Another way of including children is by *not* commenting on some things. Being aware that children are present will result, at times, in refraining from saying some things that are inappropriate for children, or altering the way some topics are expressed. Just as women's conversation changes when men are present and vice versa, so care is given when there is an awareness of who is present in the congregation on Sunday morning.

  It is helpful at all times to consider the demographics of the congregation and extend an understanding spirit as much as possible. That kind of sensitivity to the unique needs of others ministers to the whole body as we bear one another's burdens. It may lead us to recognize that Mother's Day may provoke sadness in infertile couples or those who have experienced miscarriages, and guide our remarks to appropriately care for them. In the same way that we consider the unique needs of those in the congregation, the unique needs of children should be recognized.

  For example, the manner in which statements regarding sexual situations are expressed may be altered when considering the effect on our younger members. Although this topic need not be avoided, a more delicate approach may be taken when children are present in order to preserve their innocence.

- Include children by inviting them to participate when appropriate. There are ways to include children that are meaningful, rather than "cute." Some ideas might include:

  1. Commissionings—When we huddle around missionaries to pray for them, we could specifically invite the children to come forward and pray, especially if the missionary family has children.

  2. Special Services—Including children as readers for a Christmas Eve service is a good model for children's

participation, allowing them to minister to others in the worship service. Sometimes children can lead worship through song, such as in a children's choir.

3. Serving—There may be occasions in which children can serve the body. Older children can help with the offering, pass out bulletins, or collect communion cups.

4. Testimonies—A testimony time could occasionally include a testimony from a child. Children may need to be coached in order to express a meaningful testimony, but many children have genuine answers to prayer, faith lessons learned, or experiences of God's faithfulness that would bless others given the opportunity to hear them.

5. Prayer—As we invite those to the front who have special prayer needs, it would be appropriate to also mention that any children who have a need are invited for prayer, too.

6. Recitation of Memory Verses—For churches participating in a memory verse program such as the Fighter Verses,[34] the pastor could ask a volunteer from the congregation to recite the weekly verse, and children can be encouraged to bless the body in this way.

7. Accommodate—We need to realize that it's harder to listen when we can't see the person who is preaching or singing. Just as we might provide a special spot for someone who uses a wheelchair, we might consider inviting children to come sit on the floor in the front of the sanctuary during an appropriate time, such as a baptism, so that they can easily see what is going on.

8. Cultivate a Vision—Cultivate a vision for the privilege and responsibility we have to nurture the faith of children through including them in the worship service. Create a culture in which adults don't see children as a distraction, but instead gratefully take advantage of the opportunity to encourage worship in children.

34. Fighter Verses is a Scripture memory program that can be used by individuals or groups, available from www.childrendesiringGod.org.

Intentionally teach the congregation about its responsibility to the next generation. A natural way of doing this is take advantage of the opportunity that baby dedications present to instruct members of the church that it is their responsibility to train up the next generation in the fear and instruction of the Lord.

Because we have a corporate responsibility to train the next generation, the congregation needs to be tolerant of the distractions of little children, to pray for young parents and their children, and to encourage them. By the same token, parents need to be sensitive when their children are being so distracting that they need to be removed from the service. This instruction should come from the church leaders to the church body.

9. Worship Information—When possible, have worship information available to parents before services. This could be via the church website or through a bulletin.

10. Seminars—Have a seminar for parents to give them a vision and strategy for involving their children in the worship service. Help parents to recognize the importance of bringing their children to the worship service and the mantle of responsibility they shoulder to nurture faith and worship in their children. If your church has a nursery graduation, this would be an ideal time to extend an invitation to such a seminar.

—Another source of encouragement on this topic is an interview with Pastor John Piper titled, "Should Children Sit Through 'Big Church'?" that is available online, as a transcript and as an audio recording, at http://www.desiringGod.org/interviews/should-children-sit-through-big-church.

Appendix

Suggestions for Helping Your Child Worship[35]

Sometimes the difference for children between *enduring* Sunday morning services and *enjoying* Sunday morning services is simply a matter of preparation and training. It is our heartfelt prayer that your child will come as a participant in the service to worship our great God. To that end, we have prepared a few suggestions that might help you lead your child to worship this morning.

1. **Be prepared for worship.** Sunday morning starts Saturday night. Lay out clothes (find all shoes!), get offerings ready, rehearse memory verses, gather together everything you need to bring with you, etc. before Sunday morning. Keep Sunday simple. Make a simple breakfast and leave the house with time to spare. Remind your child of your expectations of his behavior during the church service.

2. **Be a role model for your child.** Start your morning with a positive attitude, a cheerful tone, a spirit of anticipation and enthusiasm, and a heart for worship.

3. **Walk your child through the service before it starts.** Look over the bulletin.[36] Point out what will be happening and how your child can participate. This may mean teaching him a refrain of a responsive reading, or teaching him a phrase from a song or chorus and asking him to listen for it. You may also want to pray with your child before the service starts.

4. **Pray for your child.** Pray not only that your child will learn to participate and listen attentively, but that his heart would be inclined to the Lord.

5. **Encourage your child to participate in the service.** By teaching your child hymns and worship songs at home, he will be able to participate in the service. If he cannot learn the whole hymn/song, teach him the refrain and signal to him

---

35. You have permission to copy this list of suggestions.
36. If your church posts the elements of the service on its website, it will be advantageous to talk through the service at home on Saturday.

when it is time to sing the part he knows. Encourage your child to sit and to stand at the appropriate times, to clap when appropriate, etc. If you use hymn books, show him the words in the hymnbook, moving your finger along as the hymn is sung. (Even if your child is a non-reader, this will help to focus his attention and encourage him to pay attention to the words.) Have your child bring an offering and place it in the plate.

6. **Help your child become an active sermon listener.** Help your child focus on the sermon by quietly whispering instructions to him (e.g., "Listen to this story," "Can you draw a picture of...?"). This is not a time of long instruction, just very short statements to focus his attention. It is also not a time for your child to whisper back to you. Encourage a younger child to listen to the sermon and to draw a picture of something from the sermon. (This should not be seen as a time for doodling, but for active listening.) If your child is very young and has a hard time sitting for a long time, after he has listened to the sermon for a while, you may want to let your child look at small (non-distracting) Bible storybooks.

   As your child gets older and learns to write, model for him how to take simple notes. Let him copy your notes at first; eventually encourage him to take his own notes. Keep a spiral notebook that is specifically for Sunday morning, or purchase the *My Church Notebook* from Truth78 (Truth78.org).

   Put together a tote bag for your child to use specifically in church. Inside you may want to include some of the following items: small Bible storybooks, a pad of paper or notebook, Bible story coloring books or the Fighter Verse coloring book,[37] and Crayola Twistable™ crayons or colored pencils.[38]

7. **Stretch your child's ability to sit still and be attentive.** If you have an active child, you may need to take your child out of

---

37. Truth78 also offers three coloring books: *He Established a Testimony, He Has Spoken By His Son*, and the *Fighter Verses Coloring Book*, all available from Truth78.org.
38. The Crayola Twistable™ crayons tend to be less messy than other crayons, and The Crayola Twistable™ colored pencils do not need to be sharpened. Markers tend to smell and squeak, and can be more distracting to others. They can also leak, and it is easier to mark clothing, cushions, and other items with them.

the service partway through. Keep stretching the time until he can sit through the whole service. You may need to be firm. Affirm positive behavior.

8. **Talk about the service on the way home.** Speak positively with your child about the service, and ask him if he has any questions. Encourage him to share his drawings or notes.

—Another source of encouragement on this topic is an interview with Pastor John Piper titled, "Should Children Sit Through 'Big Church'?" that is available online, as a transcript and as an audio recording, at http://www.desiringGod.org/interviews/should-children-sit-through-big-church.

The Family: Together in God's Presence

by John and Noël Piper

God-centered worship is supremely important in the life of our church. We approach the Sunday morning worship hour with great seriousness and earnestness and expectancy. We try to banish all that is flippant or trivial or chatty.

Not all services are this way. Sunday morning is the Mount of Transfiguration—the awesome place of glory and speechlessness. Sunday or Wednesday evening is the Mount of Olives—the familiar spot for conversation with the Lord and each other.

In this article, we hope to do two things: 1) demonstrate that parents (or some responsible adult) should bring little children to the Sunday morning worship service rather than send them to a "children's church," and 2) give some practical advice about how to do it.

We don't claim that our way of worshipping is the only valid way. Not all our ideas may fit with the way another church does it.

For example, we don't have a children's sermon as part of our Sunday morning service. It would be fun for the children, but in the long run would weaken the spiritual intensity of our worship. To everything there is a season. And we believe that, for at least one hour a week, we should sustain a maximum intensity of moving reverence.

The Biggest Stumbling Block

There are several reasons why we urge parents to bring their children to worship. But these arguments will not carry much weight with parents who do not love to worship God.

The greatest stumbling block for children in worship is that their parents do not cherish the hour. Children can feel the difference between duty and delight. Therefore, the first and most important job of a parent is to fall in love with the worship of God. You can't impart what you don't possess.

Togetherness

Worshiping together counters the contemporary fragmentation of families. Hectic American life leaves little time for significant togetherness. It is hard to overestimate the good influence of families doing valuable things together week in and week out, year in and year out.

Worship is the most valuable thing a human can do. The cumulative effect of 650 worship services spent with Mom and Dad between the ages of 4 and 17 is incalculable.

Catch the Spirit

Parents have the responsibility to teach their children by their own example the meaning and value of worship. Therefore, parents should want their children with them in worship so the children can catch the spirit and form of their parents' worship.

Children should see how Mom and Dad bow their heads in earnest prayer during the prelude and other nondirected times. They should see how Mom and Dad sing praise to God with joy in their faces, and how they listen hungrily to His Word. They should catch the spirit of their parents meeting the living God.

Something seems wrong when parents want to take their children in the formative years and put them with other children and other adults to form their attitude and behavior in worship. Parents should be jealous to model for their children the tremendous value they put on reverence in the presence of Almighty God.

Not an Excessive Expectation

To sit still and be quiet for an hour or two on Sunday is not an excessive expectation for a healthy 6-year-old who has been taught to obey his parents. It requires a measure of discipline, but that is precisely what we want to encourage parents to impart to their children in the first five years.

Thus the desire to have children in the worship service is part of a broader concern that children be reared so that they are submissive and respectful (1 Timothy 3:4).

Children can be taught in the first five years of life to obey their father and mother when they say, "Sit still and be quiet." Parents' helplessness to control their children should not be solved by alternative services but by a renewal of discipline in the home.

Not Everything Goes Over Their Heads

Children absorb a tremendous amount that is of value. And this is true even if they say they are bored.

Music and words become familiar. The message of the music starts to sink in. The form of the service comes to feel natural. The choir makes a special impression with a kind of music the children may hear at no other time. Even if most of the sermon goes over their heads, experience shows that children hear and remember remarkable things.

The content of the prayers and songs and sermon gives parents unparalleled opportunities to teach their children the great truths of our faith. If parents would only learn to query their children after the service and then explain things, the children's capacity to participate would soar.

Not everything children experience has to be put on their level in order to do them good. Some things must be. But not everything.

For example, to learn a new language you can go step by step from alphabet to vocabulary to grammar to syntax. Or you can take a course where you dive in over your head, and all you hear is the language you don't know. Most language teachers would agree that the latter is by far the most effective.

Sunday worship service is not useless to children just because much of it goes over their heads. They can and will grow into this new language faster than we think—if positive and happy attitudes are fostered by the parents.

A Sense of Awe

There is a sense of solemnity and awe which children should experience in the presence of God. This is not likely to happen in children's church. Is there such a thing as children's thunder or children's lightning or the crashing of the sea "for children"?

A deep sense of the unknown and the mysterious can rise in the soul of a sensitive child in solemn worship—if his parents are going hard after God themselves. A deep moving of the magnificence of God can come to the young, tender heart through certain moments of great hymns or "loud silence" or authoritative preaching. These are of immeasurable value in the cultivation of a heart that fears and loves God.

We do not believe that children who have been in children's church for several years between the ages of six and twelve will be more inclined or better trained to enjoy worship than if they had spent those years at the side of their parents. In fact, the opposite is probably the case.

It will probably be harder to acclimate a 10- or 12-year-old to a new worship service than a 5- or 6-year-old. The cement is much less wet, and vast possibilities of shaping the impulses of the heart are gone.

Some Practical Suggestions from Noël

When our four sons grew to be young men, we assumed that the worship-training chapter of our life had ended. But God has wonderful surprises. Our youngest son was twelve when we adopted our daughter, who was just a couple of months old. So our experience with young children in the pew started more than twenty years ago and will continue a while longer.

Getting Started Step by Step

We discovered that the very earliest "school" for worship is in the home—when we help a baby be quiet for just a moment while we ask God's blessing on our meal; when a toddler is sitting still to listen to a Bible storybook; when a child is learning to pay attention to God's Word and to pray during family devotional times.

At church, even while our children were still nursery-aged, I began to help them take steps toward eventual regular attendance in Sunday morning worship service. I used other gatherings as a training ground—baptisms, choir concerts, missionary videos, or other special events that would grab the attention of a 3-year-old. I'd "promote" these to the child as something exciting and grown-up. The occasional special attendance gradually developed into regular evening attendance, while at the same time we were beginning to attempt Sunday mornings more and more regularly.

I've chosen not to use the church's child care as an escape route when the service becomes long or the child gets restless. I don't want to communicate that you go to a service as long as it seems interesting, and then you can go play. And I wanted to avoid a pattern that might reinforce the idea that all of the service is good, up until the preaching of God's Word—then you can leave.

Of course, there are times when a child gets restless or noisy, despite a parent's best efforts. I pray for the understanding of the people around me, and try to deal with the problem unobtrusively. But if the child won't be quiet or still, I take him or her out—for the sake of quick discipline and for the sake of the other worshippers. Then I have to decide whether we'll slip back into service or stay in the area reserved for parents with young children. It depends on how responsive the child seems and whether there's an appropriate moment in the flow of the service. If we stay in "family area" outside the sanctuary, I help my child sit quietly as if we were still in the sanctuary.

By the time they are four years old, our children assume that they'll be at all the regular weekly services with us.

Preparation All Week Long

Your anticipation and conversation before and after service and during the week will be important in helping your child learn to love worship and to behave well in service.

Help your children become acquainted with your pastor. Let them shake hands with him at the door and be greeted by him. Talk about who the worship leaders are; call them by name. Suggest that your child's Sunday school teacher invite the pastor to spend a few minutes with the children if your church's Sunday morning schedule allows for that.

If you know what the Scripture passage will be for the coming Sunday, read it together several times during the week. A little one's face really lights up when he hears familiar words from the pulpit.

Talk about what is "special" this week: a trumpet solo, a friend singing, a missionary speaker from a country you have been praying for.

Sometimes you can take the regular elements of the service and make them part of the anticipation. "We've been reading about Joseph. What do you think the pastor will say about him?" "What might the choir be singing this morning?" "Maybe we can sit next to our handicapped friend and help him with his hymn book so he can worship better too."

There are two additional and important pre-service preparations for us: a pen and notepad for "Sunday notes" and a trip to the restroom (leaving the service is highly discouraged).

What Happens During Service?

First, I let a child who wants a worship folder have one—it helps a child feel like a participant in the service. And quietly, before service begins, I may point to the different parts of the service listed in the folder.

During service, we all sit or stand along with rest of the congregation. I share my Bible or hymnal or worship folder with my little one, because use of these is an important part of the service.

The beginning of the sermon is the signal for "notetaking" to begin. (I want a child's activities to be related to the service. So we don't bring library books to read. I do let a very young child look at pictures in his Bible, if he can do it quietly.) Notetaking doesn't mean just scribbling, but "taking notes" on a special pad used just for service.

"Taking notes" grows up as the child does. At first he draws pictures of what he hears in the sermon. Individual words or names trigger individual pictures. You might pick out a word that will be used frequently in the sermon; have the child listen carefully and make a check mark in his "notes" each time he hears the word.

Later he may want to copy letters or words from the Scripture passage for the morning. When spelling comes easier, he will write words and then phrases he hears in the sermon. Before you might expect it, he will probably be outlining the sermon and noting whole concepts.

Goals and Requirements

My training for worship has three main goals:

1. That children learn early and as well as they can to worship God heartily.
2. That parents be able to worship.
3. That families cause no distraction to the people around them.

So there are certain expectations that I teach the young ones and expect of the older ones:

- Sit or stand or close eyes when the service calls for it.
- Sit up straight and still—not lounging or fidgeting or crawling around, but respectful toward God and the worshippers around you.
- Keep bulletin papers and Bible and hymnal pages as quiet as possible.
- Stay awake. Taking notes helps. (I did allow the smallest ones to sleep, but they usually didn't need to!)

- Look toward the worship leaders in the front. No people-gazing or clock-watching.
- If you can read fast enough, sing along with the printed words. At least keep your eyes on the words and try to think them. If you can't read yet, listen very hard.

Creating an Environment in the Pew

For my part, I try to create an environment in our pew that makes worship easier. In past years, I would sit between whichever two were having the most trouble with each other that day. We choose seats where we can see the front better (while seated, not kneeling on the pew; kneeling leads to squirming and blocks the view of others).

Each child has a Bible, offering money, and worship folder at hand, so he doesn't have to scramble and dig during the worship time. During the prelude, if I notice in the bulletin something unusual for which we need to be prepared (a responsive reading or congregational prayers, for example), I quietly point it out to a child who is old enough to participate.

Afterward

When the service has ended, my first words are praise to the child who has behaved well. In addition to the praise, I might also mention one or two things that we both hope will be better next time.

But what if there has been disregard of our established expectations and little attempt to behave? The first thing that happens following the service is a silent and immediate trip to the most private place we can find. Then the deserved words are spoken and consequences administered or promised.

Closeness and Warmth

On the rare occasions when my pastor-husband can sit with the rest of us, the youngest one climbs right into his lap—and is more attentive and still than usual. What a wonderful thing for a young mind to closely associate the closeness and warmth of a parent's lap with special God-times.

A child gets almost the same feeling from being next to his parent or from an arm around the shoulder or an affectionate hand on the knee.

The setting of the tight family circle focusing toward God will be a nonverbal picture growing richer and richer in the child's mind and heart as he matures in appreciation for his family and in awe at the greatness of God.

—John Piper is founder and teacher of desiringGod.org and chancellor of Bethlehem College & Seminary. For 33 years, he served as pastor at Bethlehem Baptist Church, Minneapolis, Minnesota. He is author of more than 50 books, and his sermons and articles are available online at desiringGod.org. This article is available online at desiringGod.org: http://www.desiringgod.org/articles/the-family-together-in-gods-presence.

Bibliography

Beeke, Joel R. *The Family at Church: Listening to Sermons and Attending Prayer Meetings*. (Grand Rapids, Mich.: Reformation Heritage, 2008).

Brown, Scott T. *A Weed in the Church: How a Culture of Age Segregation Is Harming the Younger Generation, Fragmenting the Family, and Dividing the Church*. (Wake Forest, North Car.: National Center for Family-Integrated Churches, 2010).

Brown, Scott T. "Is Age-Integrated Worship a Historical Norm?," posted by the National Center for Family-Integrated Churches on February 26, 2016, https://ncfic.org/blog/posts/is_age_integrated_worship_a_historical_norm.

Burk, Bud. "The Generations in the Worship Service," a seminar given at a conference in 2013 held by Truth78 (then called Children Desiring God). Audio recording: http://ethomasmedia.com/cdg/audio/2013Conference/Burk_Generations.mp3.

Ham, Ken, C. Britt. Beemer, and Todd A. Hillard. *Already Gone: Why Your Kids Will Quit Church and What You Can Do to Stop It*. (Green Forest, Ark: Master, 2009).

Helopoulos, Jason. "Children in Worship–Let's Bring It Back," posted by Kevin DeYoung, March 6, 2012, http://thegospelcoalition.org/blogs/kevindeyoung.

Michael, Sally. "Strategies for Engaging Children in the Worship Service," a seminar given at a conference in 2013 given by Truth78 (then called Children Desiring God).

Michael, Sally. "Catechism: Out-of-Date or a Tried-and-True Teaching Tool of Eternal Truths," a seminar given at a conference in 2016 given by Truth78 (then called Children Desiring God).

Piper, John. "The Children, The Church, and the Chosen," a Sunday evening sermon given at Bethlehem Baptist Church of Minneapolis, Minnesota on September 22, 1980, http://www.desiringGod.org/messages/the-children-the-church-and-the-chosen.

Piper, John. “Should Children Sit Through ‘Big Church’?” an interview with Pastor John Piper, available both as a transcript and as an audio recording at http://www.desiringGod.org/. interviews/should-children-sit-through-big-church

Piper, John and Noël. “The Family: Together in God’s Presence,” an article published January 1, 1996, http://www.desiringGod.org/articles/the-family-together-in-gods-presence.

Strange, W. A. *Children in the Early Church: Children in the Ancient World, the New Testament and the Early Church.* (Carlisle, United Kingdom: Paternoster Press, 1996).

Wright, Tim. *Sunday Schooling Our Kids Out of Church: The True Story of How One Congregation Dropped Sunday School.* (Peoria, Arizona: Tim Wright Ministries, 2015).

Wright, Tim, “Sunday Schooling Our Kids Out of Church,” posted on August 5, 2014, http://sixseeds.patheos.com/searchingfortomsawyer/2014/08/sunday-schooling-our-kids-out-of-church/.

About Truth78

Truth78 is a vision-oriented ministry for the next generations. Our vision is that the next generations know, honor, and treasure God, setting their hope in Christ alone, so that they will live as faithful disciples for the glory of God.

Our mission is to nurture the faith of the next generations by equipping the church and home with resources and training that instruct the mind, engage the heart, and influence the will through proclaiming the whole counsel of God.

Values that undergird the development of our resources and training are that they be God-centered, Bible-saturated, Gospel-focused, Christ-exalting, Spirit-dependent, doctrinally grounded, and discipleship-oriented.

Resources for Church and Home

Truth78 currently offers the following categories of resources and training materials for equipping the church and home:

Vision-Casting and Training

We offer a wide variety of booklets, video and audio seminars, articles, and other practical training resources that highlight and further expound our vision, mission, and values, as well as our educational philosophy and methodology. Many of these resources are freely distributed through our website. These resources and trainings serve to assist ministry leaders, volunteers, and parents in implementing Truth78's vision and mission in their churches and homes.

Curriculum

We publish materials designed for formal Bible instruction. The scope and sequence of these materials reflects our commitment to teach children and youth the whole counsel of God over the course of their education. Materials include curricula for Sunday schools, Midweek Bible programs, Backyard Bible Clubs or Vacation Bible Schools, and

Intergenerational studies. Most of these materials can be adapted for use in Christian schools and education in the home.

Parenting and Family Discipleship

We have produced a variety of materials and training resources designed to help parents in their role in discipling their children. These include booklets, video presentations, family devotionals, children's books, articles, and other recommended resources. Furthermore, our curricula include parent pages to help parents apply what is taught in the classroom to their child's daily experience in order to nurture faith.

Bible Memory

Our Fighter Verses Bible memory program is designed to encourage churches, families, and individuals in the lifelong practice and love of Bible memory. The Fighter Verses program utilizes an easy-to-use Bible memory system with carefully chosen verses to help fight the fight of faith. It is available in print, on FighterVerses.com, and as an app for smart phones and other mobile devices. The Fighter Verses App includes review reminders, quizzes, songs, a devotional, and other memory helps. For pre-readers, Foundation Verses uses simple images to help young children memorize 76 key verses. We also offer a study, devotional guide, and coloring book that correspond to Set 1 of the Fighter Verses. Visit FighterVerses.com for the weekly devotional blog and for free memory aids.

Nonprofit Ministry

Truth78 is a 501(c)(3) nonprofit ministry structured to tell of "the glorious deeds of the LORD, and his might, and the wonders that he has done" (Psalm 78:4) to millions of children and youth in the next generation who do not know, honor, and treasure Jesus Christ. Ministry supporters make it possible to reach more children of the next generation globally through...

- Funding curriculum translation projects that we will distribute free through our website. We have resources in numerous languages. Major translation projects are completed for 16 languages, with 15 more underway.
- Providing free training materials to equip children's and youth ministry leaders, volunteers, and parents to develop a biblical vision for their ministry to the next generation, and to provide specific training on using our resources and on the roles and functions of children's and youth ministry.
- Underwriting a fund to help ministries and individuals unable to fully afford Truth78 resources.

For more information on Truth78 or any of these initiatives, contact:

Truth:78 / Equipping the Next Generations to Know, Honor, and Treasure God

Truth78.org

info@Truth78.org

877.400.1414

@Truth78org